EXPLORING OPPOSITES

In and Out

by Joy Frisch-Schmoll

Consulting Editor: Gail Saunders-Smith, PhD

CAPSTONE PRESS
a capstone imprint

Pebble Plus is published by Capstone Press,
1710 Roe Crest Drive, North Mankato, Minnesota 56003.
www.capstonepub.com

Library of Congress Cataloging-in-Publication Data
Frisch, Joy.
 In and out / by Joy Frisch-Schmoll.
   p. cm. — (Pebble plus. Exploring opposites.)
 Includes index.
 Summary: "Full-color photographs and simple text introduce the concepts of in and out"—Provided by publisher.
 ISBN 978-1-62065-119-3 (library binding)
 ISBN 978-1-62065-897-0 (paperback)
 ISBN 978-1-4765-2123-7 (ebook PDF)
1. Picture puzzles—Juvenile literature. I. Title.

GV1507.P47F75 2013
 793.73—dc23   2012033227

Editorial Credits
Jill Kalz, editor; Ted Williams, designer; Wanda Winch, media researcher; Jennifer Walker, production specialist

Photo Credits
Alamy: Stuart Boulton, 21; Dreamstime: Fallenangel, 7, Ginger Monteleone, 15, Rebecca Abell, 17; Shutterstock: Fer Gregory,
19, Kletr, 5, lurii Konoval, cover, Matt Jeppson, 9, violetkaipa, 11, Wallenrock, 13

Note to Parents and Teachers

The Exploring Opposites set supports English language arts standards related to language
development. This book describes and illustrates the concepts of in and out. The images support
early readers in understanding the text. The repetition of words and phrases helps early readers
learn new words. This book also introduces early readers to subject-specific vocabulary words,
which are defined in the Glossary section. Early readers may need assistance to read some words
and to use the Table of Contents, Glossary, Read More, Internet Sites, and Index sections of the book.

Printed in the United States of America in North Mankato, Minnesota.
092012   006933CGS13

Table of Contents

What They Mean

What's chirping in the tree?

"In" means an object is

within or inside another object.

"Out" means an object is

outside another object.

What's In?

In and out are opposites. The yellow and blue birds sit in the cage. They eat the seeds in the trays.

A shell hides most
of a turtle's body.
The turtle can pull in
its head and legs too.

What's Out?

The goldfish look out
of the glass bowl.
One fish jumps out.

At the magic show,
a rabbit pops out
of a hat. How did it
get in?

In and Out

Tinker loves to ride

in the car.

He sticks his nose out

and sniffs the air.

Chris and Rita do

handstands in the pool.

Their heads are in the water.

Their feet are out.

You Try It: In or Out?

The mouse lives
_____ the wall.
The cat wants it
to come _____.

The elephant stands
_____ the water.
Its trunk and big ears
stick _____.

Glossary

chirp—to make a short, light sound

object—anything that can be seen and touched; a thing

opposite—as different as possible

Read More

Bogart, Jo Ellen. *Big and Small, Room for All.* Plattsburgh, N.Y.: Tundra Books of Northern New York, 2009.

Loewen, Nancy. *If You Were an Antonym.* Word Fun. Minneapolis: Picture Window Books, 2007.

Meredith, Susan Markowitz. *Half or Whole?* Little World Math Concepts. Vero Beach, Fla.: Rourke Pub., 2011.

Internet Sites

FactHound offers a safe, fun way to find Internet sites related to this book. All of the sites on FactHound have been researched by our staff.

Here's all you do:

Visit *www.facthound.com*

Type in this code: 9781620651193

Super-cool stuff! Check out projects, games and lots more at
www.capstonekids.com

Index

Word Count: 124
Grade: 1
Early-Intervention Level: 16